It's Not Goodbye

Brenda Grose

PrairieKnoll Press

Mount Ayr, Iowa

Copyright © 2019 by Brenda Grose

All rights reserved. No part of this publication may be reproduced, distributed or transmitted in any form or by any means, without prior written permission.

PrairieKnoll Press
100 Dunning Avenue
Mount Ayr, Iowa 50854

Disclaimer: All events, conversations and locales have been recreated and retold solely from the memory and perspective of the author. Some chronology may have been compressed and/or changed in keeping with the storyline at the discretion of the author. Names have not been changed, although some may have been excluded out of respect for privacy and anonymity. Any errors or omissions in fact are unintentional and every effort has been made to stay as true to the events as recollection allows.

Cover Design: Jordyn Wisroth

It's Not Goodbye/Brenda Grose
ISBN 978-1-7323970-1-9

Dedication

First and foremost, To God be the Glory.

For my son, Nick – I will never stop telling your story. I love you forever.

To my sons Chris and Mitch and to my daughters Niccole and Jordyn – this book is dedicated to you! Thank you for being my rocks, my greatest blessings, my inspiration and the ones who remind me of life, purpose and passion. May your lives be filled with happiness and joy and may you seek God in all you do. He will never fail you. I love you most.

To Jessi, Erica, Travis and Dylan – my bonus daughters and sons – thank you for being their rocks, their blessings and their inspiration. As partners, may you always remind one another of life, purpose and passion and seek God together. I love you bigger.

To the seven boys who made me a Gram, Brayden, Isaac, Dawson, Jace, Trenton, Keaton and Boston – you are the icing on the cake, another chance to watch baseballs soar, hear the crack of football pads, see feet fly on the track, basketballs find their mark, find chalk drawings on the sidewalk and see dirt moving on the "job site" under the old tree. I often see your parents and Uncle Nick in you and the reminders are sweet. May you each find your passion and purpose, follow your dreams and always keep God at your helm. I love you beyond.

To my ladies – Cherrye, Car, Carol, Misty and Shelly – you are simply the best! You keep me sane, accept my crazy, lift me up when I am down, allow me to be me, listen to my dreams, encourage my passion and go on those crazy girlfriend trips where "what happens in…stays in…" I can't imagine not having you in my life. Thank you for your love and support and for being "my people".

To my childhood friends – Angi, Karen, Ginny, Sandie and Sally – we don't get together as much as I'd like but you also have encouraged this journey and believed in my dream. Whether it is a Facebook message or just a thumbs up, your friendship is never forgotten.

To my daughter, Jordyn – who listened to my vision for the cover design and made it come true. It could not be more perfect. You are creative, intuitive and talented. Thank you thank you!

To Prairie Knoll Press and Darrell Dodge – you provided the means, the expertise and the guidance to seeing my vision in print, thank you!

From the storm clouds of loss came an awakening of faith.

God wrote the story, I just wrote the words.

Praise God from Whom all blessings flow.

This is my story.
This is my song.
Praising my Savior,
all the Day Long.
"Blesssed Assurance" 1873

Contents

Foreword 1
Forever Changed 3
Where are You, God? 13
Growing Faith 23
24 Hours 33
Trusting God's Will 43
The Things You Do 59
Celebrating Nick 81
Grief 91
A Year of Firsts 101
Hello, Last First 133
About the Author 143

Foreword

"As each has received a gift, use it to serve one another, as good stewards of God's varied Grace."
1 Peter 4:10

On January 10, 2016 at 8:35 in the morning, life as I knew it was irrevocably and forever changed. I was admitted into a club I never wished to join, only to find that club I had feared was full of kindness, compassion, understanding, acceptance and love. I was plummeted into the deepest and darkest valley I had ever experienced only to find myself uplifted by the Merciful Presence of God and wrapped tightly in His loving arms.

When life overwhelmed me and the heartache of loss seemed insurmountable, God reminded me of His goodness. When I longed for answers and pled desperately for a different script, the author of our story reminded me the story had already been written.

In my search to find understanding, to make sense of, to find purpose in the loss of my son, I found myself face to face with God. God in all His fullness, God in all His majesty, God in all His perfection. I cried out and He showed up, bigger, better and more amazingly than I could have ever imagined or hoped. In facing my greatest fear, I found the greatest gift. In loss there is hope, in death there is victory, in Heaven there is God's promise and through the gift of salvation I can rest in the absolute knowledge "It's not good-bye, it's see ya later."

1

Forever Changed

"Blessed are those who mourn, for they will be comforted."
Matthew 5:4

This is my story.

On the morning of January 10, 2016, what I then believed was my worst nightmare stood at my own front door. As I sprang out of bed to the chime of my doorbell and sprinted to the door clad only in my nightgown, I fully expected to see the grinning face of my son, Nick.

I was sure he would be pointing to a bolted door that had not been locked in forty years and indignantly and teasingly asking, "You locked me out?"

I was already formulating my response, "You said you'd be home last night, Mister," as I rounded the corner from my bedroom and caught sight of our lanky town sheriff through the glass door.

My stomach tightened instantly – the sheriff in uniform at the door was usually not a good sign. Suddenly shaking, I hesitantly opened the door.

"Hi, Mike," I said with an unspoken question in my trembling voice.

His words were sharp swords swiftly and calmly delivered, although I noted his watery eyes. When he cleared his throat, I knew it was bad.

"I'm sorry to tell you, Nick had a car accident and he passed away."

"What? Noooooooo," I moaned, "please, no."

I crumpled to the floor as my world crumbled around me. My cherished, precious son was gone. I could not even process the words. Nausea welled up as my stomach churned and I believe in that instant I truly felt the shattering of my heart into a million pieces inside my chest. I held my head in my hands and sobbed.

Our sheriff became just Mike in those moments, a kid who grew up with my kids. I know Mike chose to be the one to deliver the news, although he could have passed it off to a deputy. I'm sure it was probably one of the harder calls he would ever make, but I'm so thankful it was Mike at that door. He knelt beside me and wrapped those Sheriff Mike arms around me and asked who he should call. It was clear he was not leaving until someone arrived. I mumbled out the names of my oldest son and my son-in-law as the tears streamed relentlessly and then I sat...in that same place I had fallen...and I waited...and I wept. As I write these words, I am reminded of the shortest verse in the Bible, *"Jesus wept."* **John 11:35.**

Jesus wept as he entered the city of Jerusalem. He had come to raise Lazarus from death, but he knew the greater task that lay before Him at the cross. In that moment, Jesus did the most human thing. He wept. He wept not for himself, not for the torture and agony that awaited His human self as He took OUR sin, but out of great compassion. He wept out of great, big, amazing and incomprehensible love for the loss being felt that minute, even though He knew it would be changed to joy when Lazarus was raised up. He weeps for and along with us, too, through every tear we cry.

I believe that as I wept that day, and Jesus and the angels rejoiced as they welcomed my son home, there was also weeping in the heavens for the enormity of grief and the journey that lay before me and my family. From the very beginning, God was there.

In a small town and the huge world of social media, news travels fast. The news of tragedy travels even faster. It was important to let my daughters, Niccole and Jordyn, and sons, Chris and Mitch, know first. Sheriff Mike would take care of contacting my three who lived in town, but I worried about Jordyn, two hours away at Iowa State University in Ames, Iowa. I would have chosen to tell her in person, but I knew she would have to be told over the phone. The last thing I wanted was for her to read it on Facebook. I gave Mike the numbers of her closest college friends to ask them to be with her when we called.

As Mike quietly placed those calls, I sat in a fog of great, gasping tears stilled intermittently by silent numbness when my body demanded reprieve. I couldn't wrap my mind around what I had just heard. The words were brutal and final. Nothing made sense and reality was just too painful to accept.

Chris and wife, Jessi, their sons, Isaac and Jace, Niccole, her husband, Travis and their boys, Brayden, Dawson, Trenton and Keaton and Mitch and Erica, my precious family, arrived within minutes. Jordyn had been contacted and a friend was driving her home. We were a sobbing, broken band of sorrow and disbelief. We held one another like shipwrecked victims clinging desperately to a single life raft in the midst of a raging storm.

The news did quickly spread and so began a steady stream of food, condolences, hugs, Nick stories and sometimes just silent comfort. Friends showed up to take command of the food and flow of traffic and to hold me together. I functioned in numbness, greeting people who came to the door and comforting them as they also comforted me. I offered cake and cookies, a sandwich...I did anything that seemed remotely normal in this new completely abnormal realm.

I talked, I smiled, I laughed, I cried...all while inside I felt nothing, just a huge yawning nothingness. Sometimes I felt completely removed from the activity around me, as though I was invisible or watching from a distance. Other times I became an actor in my own horror movie.

I have come to believe God created the mind to be protected from unspeakable heartache or pain. My mind and I were existing in that place of protection that I now recognize as the covering of

Grace. I really think the loss of a child is simply so much to bear that God, as a parent, filters what we feel for a time, until we are able to feel and process from a stronger place of existence.

Time moved without notice and soon it was night. The ache was physical and overwhelming. I had gone to bed, as instructed by well-meaning friends and family, but sleep was the farthest thing from my mind. The night before...that last night, and the two months prior kaleidoscoped through my mind as I remembered November 2015…

2

Where are You, God?

The Lord is close to the brokenhearted and saves those who are crushed in spirit.
Psalm 34:18

What began the middle of November 2015 came to be some of the worst days and some of the best days our family has ever experienced together. They would become hard lessons learned and precious memories. It began with a simple phone call on a chilly Friday afternoon, from my middle son, Nick. He asked if I was home and I replied I was, puzzled that he was calling in the middle of the day when he should be working. He told me he was coming by and I waited somewhat apprehensively.

Nick and I had always been close, so the fact that he called and needed to talk wasn't that unusual, but in the middle of a work day, I assumed it must be something very important.

About twenty minutes later Nick walked through my door. The look on his face told me, something was terribly wrong.

"She left," he said.

"What do you mean, she left? Why, what happened?" I asked shocked.

IT'S NOT GOODBYE

He told me the story, grim faced and struggling to fight back tears. His wife of four years had arrived at his jobsite and told him she was leaving him. Nick was stunned, full of questions that had no answers and hurt. There was no talking about it, according to what Nick understood. He had left that morning for work with an "I love you, see you tonight" and by afternoon she was gone.

Apparently, it was over...just like that. I listened and when he was done, he looked at me, with a weak grin and said, "I always know where I can come."

In that moment, Nick was simply my child. And in that moment, I took that child, that grown man, my son, in my arms and let him sob out the ache of his heart. Tears, even grown man tears, are not the sign of weakness, they are the sign of a big heart. Nick had one of the biggest.

"We will get through this as a family," I assured him, and he nodded and sank back into the couch. With the weight of the world on his shoulders he sat in silence.

The following weeks as Nick went through the aftermath of his broken marriage, the texts back and forth, the attempts to reconcile and the rejection, loss and abandonment, he wore the shield of the "no tears, tough guy, man's man" in public. Behind the scenes, he was broken.

In a world where partners and spouses come and go as often as the tide rolls in and out, and marriage is no longer held sacred, this may seem to some to be "no big deal." It was a big deal for Nick.

Nick moved into my house with me while he tried to sort his life out. Emotionally, he couldn't return to the house he and his wife had shared although it sat empty. It was too full of memories. Jeremy, our "adopted" Missouri son, was also staying at my house during his winter lay off, another friend for Nick to rely on and to be part of many late night conversations.

The first couple of days after the announcement that hit Nick square between the eyes, he simply paced. He paced so long I was sure he would truly wear holes in the floor. H paced and he questioned, why? He paced and shook his head, he paced and repeated the same questions over and over, sometimes I think just to keep from thinking. He didn't understand, but more than that he was hurt and felt helpless to do anything about the situation. He wore out the "what if's" and "if only's" and I had no answers. Long days and even longer nights became our life and the goal was simply to get through each day as his new reality set in.

Crisis really does separate the true and trusted from the occasional and Nick's crisis was no exception. The true and trusted stepped up. Friends stopped by the house, sent texts to Nick and invited him out. Crisis can also prove the grit and bonds of family. Nick's family, his brothers, sisters and nephews surrounded Nick with love. I have never been as proud of them as I was during that incredibly tough time. They gave up their own sleep to sit with their brother, came at the drop of a hat when called, no matter the time. They didn't question Nick, try to fix Nick or try to persuade him what he was feeling was wrong. They were simply, but so powerfully...there.

From 800 miles away, Nick's Aunt Shelly, my sister, prayed for him incessantly and texted him daily. From that same 800 miles away, his Uncle Donnie, his dad's brother, reached out with phone calls and words of reassurance, "it will get better, it will work out, I understand."

We also knew, it was a "big deal."

I have to be honest, as the days turned into weeks, my body was tired and my mind was frazzled and my heart was worn watching the heartache I could not fix. I longed for rest and for the tide to turn, for normalcy to return to our family, for things to simply get better. My own faith was being tested and it was stretched thin. As I prayed for Nick and for God's plan to be revealed to him in a mighty way, I prayed just as hard for my own faith. I prayed for unwavering trust and unshakeable faith that God was working in Nick's life. That trust provided an unexplainable hopefulness in the midst of the physical weariness to see it all play out. To that I clung through the continued weeks.

Over and over, the love flowed to Nick. In fact, I am sure that Nick had never been so "loved without ceasing" as he was during that time of darkness. The love began to do its work and Nick began to heal. While Nick was starting to truly believe God was listening, in true Nick fashion he also began to question the timing of his answers.

At one point, in frustration, Nick asked, "When am I going to see these great things God has planned for me?"

His impatience was showing, and I reminded him again of God's perfect timing although inside, I too, was praying feverishly and asking for a sign for Nick, for something for him to hold onto.

"Well, he knows I'm impatient," he replied.

It was so true I laughed, "Oh, son, he most definitely does know your impatience, he knows everything about you!"

"You have searched me, Lord, and you know me. You know when I sit and when I rise, you perceive my thoughts from afar ... You are familiar with all my ways."
Psalms 139:1-3

3

Growing Faith

"He refreshes my soul. He guides me along the right paths for his name's sake."
Psalms 23:3

As the weeks passed, we started to see "our Nick" again. His old smile returned, he found his tongue-in-cheek sense of humor and he renewed old and trusted friendships. He began going out with friends, was back to work and he had met a girl who loved his dog and made him laugh. It was a laugh I hadn't heard in a very long time.

Things were coming together for Nick in his daily life, but more importantly, he was growing a heart for God. He began to pray regularly and as he drew closer to God, he wanted to understand more about faith, about God's promises, about what He wanted for Nick's life and of course, when He was going to answer Nick's prayers. Did I mention Nick's lack of patience?

During those talks, that we called "campfires" and often included Jeremy, I would see a glimmer of the 16-year-old Nick. At 16, he had always had questions, always wanted to understand things and in many late-night talks as that 16-year-old, the subject of faith came up. I can still see him sprawled one night across the end of my bed. He was going through a tough time and I was trying to explain to him that everyone goes through those times. I always called them our "valleys."

He had listened and thought and then, I can hear him saying these words so clearly yet today, "You know mom, I guess, if we never went through a valley, how would we ever appreciate a mountaintop?"

Pretty wise words from a 16-year-old mostly focused on girls and sports and testing the limits. And Nick was that son who sorely tested my limits and went one step beyond. He not only veered off the path God wrote for him but careened recklessly down completely opposite roads. He challenged and wore me out with his debating skills and hoodwinked me a time or twenty with his magnetic sideways grin.

I always believed though, that Nick carried the heart of a lion. He loved big and he loved hard. I prayed my rule-breaking, boundary-crossing, lionhearted child would grow to be a man of lion-sized character, heart and most importantly, a man of God. While he was growing into that man, I prayed for his protection and my patience and occasionally I just prayed for a good night's sleep! Need I add, the teen years were rough?

During the months of November and December 2015, Nick was in the deepest valley he had ever faced, and he needed a mountaintop experience and the support of those who loved him.

We have always been a close-knit family and because we live so close to one another, we always did a lot together as a family.

From November 2015 to January 2016, we spent even more time together. We had family suppers and family game nights. We got together for Nick and for no reason at all, except that we seemed to be drawn to soaking up time together. That Christmas, at our traditional Pajama Party Christmas Night, Nick won a raucous Candy Cane pickup game, Chris and Jessi claimed honors for the best Gingerbread House amidst the teasing accusations of "rule breaking" and we later called it one of the best Christmases ever. It was as though we were cramming memories in on a deadline and in fact, we were doing just that.

As Nick's faith grew, he confided to me that as the middle son he didn't feel like he had ever led his two brothers in anything. Chris as the oldest, was by nature and birth order, the leader of his two brothers. He led them in athletic accomplishments through school. He led them both into their careers of sculpting the land as only a true "dirt man" can do and he led them in character. Although one of Nick's immediate goals was to lead the family in prayer as we gathered for a meal together, his greater goal was to lead Chris and Mitch into a closer relationship with God. I didn't know then how that would happen, but I had complete trust that it would.

Nick came home one night in early December 2015, with a quote, sent by a friend. The quote read, "The devil whispers you cannot withstand the storm, the warrior replies I AM the STORM."

He showed it to me and said with determination and boldness, "I want to be that warrior."

Ever the optimist, I assured him he would be, and he grinned. I always believed Nick had a calling he hadn't yet found, but I began to believe it with a bold certainty as the days wore on. I searched for scriptural assurance and was led to the book of Jeremiah.

"Before I formed you in the womb, I knew you. Before you were born, I set you apart. I anointed you as a prophet to the nations."
Jeremiah 1:5

In no way am I implying Nick was born to be a prophet like Jeremiah, but the scripture reminded me that we are all known to God before we are born. The scripture tells us He sets us apart with a unique role He has chosen. We aren't accidental or coincidental! The role God chooses for us may certainly be that as a prophet as it was for Jeremiah or it may be as a warrior as I believe it was to be for Nick. What I didn't know about Nick's role was just how soon he would become that warrior.

The quote shared by Nick and the scripture from the book of Jeremiah played through my head, as I lay in my bed that first night after the accident. I thought back to all that had happened since that day in November and I began to see so clearly the true gift God had been preparing for Nick. Beginning to understand God's great plan brought comfort, but it didn't stop the tears and the sadness

IT'S NOT GOODBYE

and the simple, aching longing for Nick as I continued to lay quietly in the darkness of the night.

4

24 Hours

"He heals the broken-hearted and binds up their wounds."
Psalms 137:3

Sleep continued to elude me as my mind replayed the day, January 10. It had now been less than 24 hours. Less than 24 hours and yet, everything in my entire world had changed and even the language used in conversation would change. Time would be forever split and we would refer to it in terms of "before the accident" and "after", to "when Nick was here" and "now" without him, to "when our family was whole" and to "now," a family newly broken. In a simple split second of time, we had become a family forever missing a piece of their own unique puzzle.

Staring into the dark night, my body was exhausted, but my mind would still not shut down. All the things that had once seemed so ordinary took on the role of "last" memories. I could see Nick's smile and the crooked grin that could steal hearts, win friends and persuade softhearted moms. I could feel Nick's trademark hug, strong and warm and I could see the jaunty wave of his hand as he strolled out the door, that last night.

"Why don't you stay in tonight, bud?" I had somewhat teasingly asked before he left.

Niccole, Travis and their boys were visiting, and we were all set to watch a new movie that went along with the Bible study Nick had wanted to start with his family. It was "War Room." I didn't even know what a war room was (a solitary place chosen for prayer), but I would soon find myself seeking solace in that very place.

"Hey, mama, I've got friends waiting," he'd replied as he gave me a hug.

I smiled and said, "I'll see ya later. Be careful. I love you."

"Love ya, too," Nick smiled.

"Will you be home tonight?" I'd asked, at the last minute, always the mom.

"I'll be home, tonight. I promise," he replied, and he hugged me one more time. It would be my last hug.

After Nick left that night, we watched the movie. Later, Niccole, Travis and their boys went home, and I fell asleep and slept soundly, which was unusual when Nick was not home.

When he had come back to stay, I had taken on old habits from when my kids were teenagers. I would lay awake or drift in and out of sleep until I heard footsteps on the front porch and the soft creak of the door opening. When I could hear he was settled in and sleeping, then I would go to sleep.

A strange thing happened that night that was more significant than I realized at the time. I woke up and looked over at a clock on my nightstand. The bright red numerals showed 3:48 a.m. As I was looking at the time, I felt something brush my shoulder. I thought nothing of it and went peacefully back to sleep.

What is strange is that I do not have a clock on my nightstand. The even stranger part is that it was later determined Nick probably passed away somewhere around that time. Some will say it was coincidence, others will write it off as a dream or wishful thinking. As for me, Nick would never leave without saying good-bye. God was there from the moment Nick was conceived and before and was there the moment he was called home. He too, knew Nick would not leave without saying goodbye.

As I tossed and turned restlessly in my bed, and the jumble of thoughts continued assaulting my mind, I remembered another conversation Nick and I had about God's gifts. I had confidently told him that God only gives His very best gifts to those who are prepared to recognize the gift, receive the gift and take care of the gift. I went on to advise Nick that he would have to do the work in his heart to receive that amazing gift from God.

I had no inkling that God was preparing Nick for the gift of salvation. I never even considered it would be God's greatest and eternal gift. In my shortsightedness and human "momness," I was sure He was going to send someone to Nick to be his partner, someone to love him and share his life. I was already seeing babies in his arms and mini Nick's slinging ball bats over their shoulders. I just knew Nick was going to have an absolutely wonderful life ahead of him and we would all get to watch it unfold!

I grimace now at how I set my sights on the things of this world and hold them in such high esteem, forgetting the things of Heaven that are so very much bigger, better and eternal. I had no idea that in the early morning hours of January 10, 2016, God would be receiving Nick into his heavenly kingdom, but God knew. God not only knew, He loved my son, Nick, so much that He purposefully used what Nick saw as his greatest heartbreak to prepare him for the incredible gift I kept promising was coming.

It's what God does. He doesn't cause harm or pain. He doesn't cause sickness or heartache. He doesn't cause sin or destruction or bad things, at all. What He does do is this- He take the brokenness, the dark moments, the lost situations, the poor choices- OUR broken pieces and He recreates them into beautiful mosaics of life. He does it because He loves us. And He saves the best for last, our eternity in Heaven with Him. Our time here is always working toward our time there, with God and God determines that time.

"Man's dates are determined: you (God) have decreed the number of his months and have set limits he cannot exceed."
Job 14:5

God determines that time, when we are born and when we go home to heaven and He determines it long before we arrive and not according to our will but according to His.

As clearly as it became in the days following Nick's death that God had been preparing him to be received into Heaven, it began to dawn on me, God had been preparing me for that day as well, as far back as a windy day in March, two scared young parents and one strong willed infant – all three fighting for that child's life. As always, God was there. And I remember… Wyoming, March 1985.

5

Trusting God's Will

"I prayed for this child, and the Lord has granted me what I asked of Him. So now, I give him to the Lord."
Samuel 1:27-28

Nick was born, Nicholas Daniel Grose on March 3, 1985, in Casper, Wyoming. He was a 21-week gestational/28-week fetal preemie according to his many medical records. Nick was delivered in an emergency Cesarean section due to a condition called placenta abruptia. Although he was tiny, right from the start our pediatrician, Dr. Joe, called him his little "warrior". Funny that all those years earlier, a doctor had used those exact words to describe our little fighter, or perhaps…. not a coincidence at all. Without us even realizing it, God was there.

What we could see even then, was that Nick's feistiness was his strength as he battled to build up his lungs and gain weight, along with keeping his vitals status quo. Nick came home after three weeks in the Casper Medical Center. My husband, Kenny, and I settled into family life in the nearby town of Glenrock, Wyoming, with our two older children, Niccole, 7, and Chris, 5, and our new baby, Nicholas. Life was perfect.

When Nick was around seven weeks old, I made a doctor's appointment based on a gut feeling that something was not right with him. Dr. Joe found nothing in his exam and reassured me it was just my heightened "preemie mom" caution. That same night, I awoke in our bedroom to an icy chill in the air and a voice saying, "Check the baby." I didn't even question the voice in our bedroom, as I immediately reached out to the cradle at our bedside and laid my hand on Nick's back to feel his breathing. I couldn't feel the steady rise and fall on his little back. I jumped out of bed, grabbed Nick from the cradle and began running hysterically around the house. Did I mention I am not really good in a crisis?

Looking back, if it hadn't been so scary, it would have been comical. Our house was one in which you could circle the main living area. As I ran circling, screaming incoherently and crying...Kenny was chasing me trying to find out what was wrong. As it was, all that jostling actually loosened the heavy congestion in Nick's lungs and he suddenly started crying and we knew he was breathing again.

Long story short, 911 was called, we were transported to the Casper hospital by ambulance and a few hours later Nick was life flighted to Denver Children's Hospital in Denver, Colorado, the nearest large hospital with a Pediatric ICU. I rode with Nick and Kenny drove to Denver and arrived later. The diagnosis: Respiratory syncytial virus – RSV.

RSV is not always so serious, our doctors explained, but our son's tiny lungs were compromised by being premature and this cold like virus was serious for Nick. All they could do was keep him on oxygen and breathing treatments and keep him monitored until the virus ran its course.

In the flurry of activity with the ambulance and paramedics earlier that night, Niccole and Chris had been whisked off to a friend's house with little explanation and Kenny and I arrived in Denver with only the clothes we were wearing.

Day 2 in the Pediatric ICU, Nick had improved enough to allow Kenny and I a chance to go back home and get more clothes and check on our kids. We knew they must be worried and scared.

Given the okay to head back home we gathered what little we had and headed out. We planned to pick up Niccole and Chris, spend the night and the next day at home with them and then head back to Denver late the next afternoon.

As we crawled into bed after the six-hour trip home and picking up the kids from a nearby neighbor's house, we were tired but relieved to be home for a few hours. Nick was where he needed to be and getting the best care possible. We fell into an exhausted sleep and were wakened abruptly to the ringing of our phone only hours later.

I groggily answered, Hello?"

"Mrs. Grose?" the voice asked.

"Yes," I answered with concern. It was the middle of the night and my inner alarms instantly chimed in high panic.

"This is Denver Children's Hospital. Nicholas has taken a downturn and you need to return as soon as possible."

My voice trembled as I asked, "How bad?"

"He's experiencing some trouble with his lungs. We advise you to come as soon as possible," the nurse replied.

My memory is paraphrasing this exact conversation, but the message received was clear. Nick had gotten bad and we needed to get to the hospital, ASAP.

Relaying the information to Kenny who sat looking at me questioningly, we began to throw clothes and things (whatever we could grab) into a suitcase and called my mom to come stay with the kids we had put to sleep in their own beds only hours before. We had not gotten to really talk to them about their brother and we were leaving again, in the middle of the night.

Fearing the six-hour road trip would not be soon enough, we called the airport in Casper and arranged the next flight out to Denver. Getting to the airport and on to the plane, I don't even remember. I was, no doubt, gripped with fear and anxious to get to my baby son. What I do remember clearly was a moment when looking out at the clouds we were flying through I began reciting a demanding mantra: "Please, don't let him die, please don't let him die." I was pleading with God for my son's life, demanding at first and then begging, as that plane dropped slowly to the airport runway, then taxied to our terminal.

Suddenly out of nowhere or somewhere I had not even known existed in my mind, I was struck with words I did not want to speak mere seconds before they came boldly out of my mouth. I sat back, took a deep breath and a quiet pause from my relentless prayer and surrendered my will to God's with these words, "He was your child first, God. I ask that Your Will be done, whatever it is, but please, God, make me strong enough to handle it."

I felt a strange calm and quietness as we disembarked from our flight and drove our rented car to the hospital.

To preface where I was at in my faith at that time, I believed in God, had been raised in church and knew Bible stories, the ones that all kids learn. I didn't really have a deep personal relationship with God, but I knew enough to pray when things were bad, and I believed God could do anything.

I look back envisioning how I kept God on a shelf, you know, for emergencies and such. I'd just pull him down from that shelf when I needed him and the rest of the time, He didn't get much, if any of my time or thought. I could do life pretty well on my own, right? How young and arrogant I was and how merciful and loving was God.

IT'S NOT GOODBYE

We walked through the first doors into the pediatric ICU and as we washed up in the outer area, we could see the isolette where we had last seen Nick. It was surrounded by medical staff, but we couldn't see Nick. As we pushed through the second set of doors a nurse turned toward us wearing the strangest expression. I stopped in my tracks, expecting, but somehow accepting the worst.

"What's going on?" I asked.

"We don't know," she answered.

The statement was simple, and I could read the disbelief and wonder on her face. A couple of the nurses turned to us and as they moved from the tight circle they had formed, we could see our baby boy, kicking and moving and I was immediately at his side touching and caressing him.

"What happened?" I again asked.

Nick's nurse, the one assigned only to him, spoke up.

"Honestly, it was something I have never seen before. I was here with your baby, monitoring his vitals and watching him. He was ashen with some blue around his lips and his extremities. We took him to X-ray," she went on to explain," and it showed his lungs were collapsed, all but a tiny pocket. That's when we called you."

Seeing my confused look as I gently touched the soft little toes and stroked Nick's downy head, the nurse continued, "That's where it got, well...we didn't know what was happening. As I stood here monitoring, I saw his toes begin to get pink and then his fingertips. I called another nurse over to look, too."

The nurses, a doctor and an X-ray tech still standing there were nodding their heads as she filled us in.

"We rushed him back to x-ray. It was crazy. The X-rays had completely reversed in the image we saw. Where we had seen complete collapse before, we now saw complete inflation in his lungs. The one small pocket of air he had relied on was now the only spot in his lungs that was deflated. I really have no idea what happened," she finished.

I looked up, smiled and replied, "I do."

Imagine that? All those years before, God was there.

For the first time in my life I had surrendered my will to God's. I didn't even understand the enormity of that moment, or what surrendering will really mean, but I knew God had answered my prayer, with just the answer I wanted. To underscore the reality of this miracle, God had even left, what I later called "his calling card" - an X-ray that showed a complete reverse image of what had been seen only hours before. God's handprint was unmistakable.

To clear up any misconceptions, God didn't miraculously save Nick because he was more deserving than another baby, he did not miraculously save him because of anything we had done or not done. God showed us a miracle because it was part of His greater plan for Nick, a plan we will never fully know or understand here on Earth.

In the wake of being witness to a miracle, you would expect to hear how that miracle changed our lives. You might expect to hear how our faith grew from a little faith to a huge faith. You might even assume we gave our lives, 100 %, right then and there to God, so thankful for the gift of that incredible miracle.

I wish I could tell a wonderful faith story like that, but I'm ashamed to say, that's not at all what happened. As thankful as I was to have my baby out of danger and on the mend, as thankful as I was that he continued to improve and was soon ready to go home, I did none of those things. Kenny and I went back to our perfect lives, with our three perfect children, in our perfect brand-new house and God was returned to the shelf, waiting until I needed Him again.

Although I had briefly surrendered my will concerning Nick's fate during those crucial hours when his life hung in the balance, it was not even close to what I have now found is true surrender.

My journey of faith; however, had experienced a first touch and years later as I began to grow my faith, through other people and other touches, I looked back on that time and realized it was my beginning. The lessons I learned? First of all, I learned that in all my imperfections, when my faith is a little or a lot, regardless of what I do God does not change and He doesn't leave. As we stumbled through those next few days after Nick's passing, God was there.

6

The Things You Do

"Even though I walk through the valley of the shadow of death, I will fear no evil for you are with me. Your rod and your staff, they comfort me."
Psalms 23:4

There are things that must be done when a loved one passes. Those very tasks are the first evidence that life does indeed continue to move forward. They are also steps that provide a way to show honor and respect, a way to remember with funny stories and reminders of precious milestone events and they are steps to the inevitable return to life, something at the time, I thought would never be possible.

On the second day after Nick's passing it was time to set down and make funeral decisions. Our friend, pastor and funeral director, Bill guided us through the list of decisions with kindness and empathy. We sat as a group in our basement, Travis and Niccole, Chris and Jessi, Mitch and Erica, Jordyn and their dad, Kenny and his wife, Janet.

As we sat around that circle trying to get comfortable with the conversation we would have,

Bill commented about the wristband Nick was wearing the night of the accident. It was actually one that Nick never took off. The wristband was true Denver Bronco fan colors of orange and blue, worn to honor his late Uncle Jim and it bore the inscription 'Proverbs 29:25':

"Fear of man will prove to be a snare, but whoever trusts in the Lord is kept safe."

Nick always loved his Uncle Jim, but he had come to look up to him even more as he watched Jim's walk through the minefield of cancer. Jim lost his battle with cancer but he never lost his faith in God. The wristband, the reminder of Jim's own battle was very important to Nick.

To show just how Nick valued that wristband, anyone who knows Nick knows he was always a sharp dresser, and his choice of clothes always "matched." Nick wore that wristband to a friend's wedding where he was dressed in the chosen wedding colors of purple and black and also his Denver Bronco orange and blue wristband. The sacrifice of fashion for Nick revealed just how close to his heart Nick carried those words and his Uncle Jim.

Bill's comment was, "A man goes out dressed for a Saturday night with a wristband that has 'Proverbs 29:25' written on it, that man knows Jesus!" made it clear he, too understood the significance of that wristband and he recognized the evidence of Nick's growing faith.

As a family, we had been witnessing heightened signs of God's presence and His plan for

Nick most notably the two months before his passing. The fact that Nick's passing was in God's hands and in God's timing continued to be apparent as our discussion and decision making for his services began.

Most thirty-year-olds would not have talked of plans in the event of their passing. Amazingly, we as a family, knew exactly what Nick's wishes would be.

Chris and Mitch knew the songs Nick would want played and quickly listed them. I briefly caught my breath and looked hesitant at one of the songs, "Drink a Beer."

I just didn't think it was "church" appropriate, but my grown children quickly called me out: "You are just worried about what people will think."

They were right. I hadn't heard the song; it was the word *beer*. As though the fact that Nick liked his Coors Light was a secret?

"It is what Nick would have wanted," they said firmly, unwavering on the selection, "besides, you haven't even heard it."

Convicted, I nodded my consent and made a mental note to listen to the song before it was played at Nick's service. I realized in that moment how often I've worried what others think and how often I haven't worried about what God thinks. I have learned what God thinks is a lot more important!

IT'S NOT GOODBYE

Niccole and Jordyn knew exactly what Nick should wear. He loved the Northface vest I had given him for his 30th birthday and wore it often. He was wearing it that night. They chose the vest and a blue shirt because blue was his favorite color.

We discussed the idea of a visitation or not, open casket or closed, burial or cremation. One thing we learned as parents with a large family; our children had needs in the loss of their brother as much as we, his parents.

A concern for our family was seeing Nick for the first time after the accident. Although I had initially wanted to see Nick when I was told of his accident, I was advised very gently to wait until Bill, our friend and funeral director had "gotten him ready."

Our first "look" then, would be in the funeral home and traditionally in a casket. It was just too soon for that stark reality. Jordyn was the first to speak up and because we had that friend, Bill, who was also the funeral director, Bill listened. Jordyn didn't want to see her brother, at least for this first time, in a casket. Bill did not hesitate to honor our wishes.

Instead of a casket, Nick lay on a discreetly disguised gurney and was covered by his Grandma Barb's handmade afghans. One afghan depicted Nick in his high school football jersey in running action. The second had the logo of his favorite college football team - the Iowa Hawkeyes - woven into the design. Covered by his grandma's love could not have been more perfect.

IT'S NOT GOODBYE

We went together as a family that first time. There was hesitance, there was fear of the unknown, there was sadness, but there was also a need to see our beloved Nick. It was uncharted territory as we approached and there was a certain initial awkwardness.

Something our family has always understood is how to come together as a family. Although it was hard, although it was nothing we had ever imagined doing, as a family we encircled our son, brother and uncle. There were whispered questions and tentative touches as we drew closer. For me, it was my son and I caressed his face and brow, permanently embedding that touch in my mind.

Being the first to reach out, I was caught up in the moment of my own emotion. Keaton, however, noticed Jordyn's hesitation to actually touch Nick's body and as a 5-year-old, accepted the challenge.

He boldly reached up and touched Nick's hand. "See, I did it," he stated.

As a child he wasn't afraid and to him, it was just Nick. His innocent gesture broke the invisible wall of propriety and suddenly we were just Nick's family, loving him, talking to him, touching him and soaking in the last look at that beautiful vessel that had carried the soul and heart of our incredible, amazing, beloved Nick. We knew Nick's soul was not there, but the human vessel we had loved for a long time was. Saying "good-bye" to that part of our life would prove to be beyond hard but together we clung and navigated our new journey.

For anyone wondering how they might react faced with the reality of the loss of a loved one, I am reminded of one of the first rules I learned about loss…there are no rules. If you are not comfortable with up close and personal, it's okay. If you need that touch and time, it's okay. If you need to talk about it or not talk about it, if you need to be surrounded by friends and family or to grieve in solitary quietness, if you have unrealistic but momentary ideas about not physically giving up that amazing vessel that stored your loved one's very essence and keeping that vessel with you…know that you are not alone.

It's all okay…the crazy feelings, the desperate pleading, the numbing pain of nothingness, whatever you are feeling, they are your feelings and they WILL and DO demand to be felt. Give yourself permission to do just that.

As we continued to discuss arrangement decisions, not one person seated in that circle questioned that Nick's choice was to be cremated. I was hesitant from a Christian standpoint to agree to his wishes. Kenny and I had been raised to believe only burial was allowed. I sat quietly contemplating how to respond and I could see the reluctance on Kenny's face as well. While we agreed to cremation that day, I knew I would have to get to my Bible and go to God in prayer to find answers and peace with that decision.

Again, for those who may have faced or might face that same question, know that you are not alone. It is a hard question. Knowing that Nick had been adamant about cremation, I had to know if honoring his wishes would dishonor God. I searched for Biblical direction and found that God gives no absolute directives, although google provides hundreds of answers. I was satisfied with finding no absolute commandment forbidding cremation and knew that all we did and would do for Nick in these final acts would be out of respect and great love. The manner we ultimately chose for laying him to rest would not determine his place in heaven.

On this subject, I would say, do the research, seek a biblical perspective if you need to know what

God says, search your own heart and consider the wishes of your loved one.

God can take a particle and make a man; He will have no problem resurrecting your loved one from cremains or the natural decomposition of bones. Sometimes it is important to remember, what we do to honor our loved ones when they pass, is often as much for those left behind as the loved one gone on. Most of all, be at peace with your decision.

While we had made the necessary service arrangements, I must admit my heart was not at peace. Accepting Nick was gone was simply too painful and I continued to exist in that state of nothingness while I pretended I was "doing just fine."

I mentioned earlier that my revelation of the true meaning of surrender came a few days into the first week. To be exact, it was day three, the third day after Nick's passing and the next morning after our meeting with Bill.

My cell phone rang around 8:00 a.m. and I answered. It was the state medical examiner asking for identifying marks and questions about Nick before doing the mandated autopsy on Nick. He had passed away alone, in a one vehicle accident, the autopsy was required by law.

As early as it was, only Jeremy, was there along with Karen, my friend who had come to be with me. I handed the phone to Jeremy and began crying. It was another cold blow of reality. Could there really be this many tears in the human body? I would find out that, yes, yes there are that many and many more.

"I can't talk to him," I mumbled.

As I heard Jeremy on the phone answering questions, it hit me what day it was and what this man was about to do to my son. It was the third day after Nick's passing. The third day. The third day was extremely significant as a Christian and a glimmer of hope rose up in me. While to some it might seem like pure lunacy, hysteria or simple denial of the facts…to me, it was the third day and amazing, miraculous things can happen on the third day.

I turned to Jeremy and yelled at him, "Don't let him touch my son, don't let him touch my son!"

IT'S NOT GOODBYE

My friend, Karen, looked alarmed as she sat by me patting my hand and I suspect searching the room frantically for help. I began to plead with God to resurrect my son. He did it for his own son, He could do it for mine. I repeated those words over and over, persistent and demanding, crying, begging, reminding...as Jeremy completed the phone call out of my earshot and Karen continued to try and calm me.

Suddenly, everything and everyone physically in that room vanished. As clear as day, I saw Jesus. He was surrounded by light with outstretched hands, kind of like the pictures that I remember from childhood. Beside him I could see my son Nick, lying on a gurney wearing what he had left in that Saturday night.

While I make no claim as a visionary, and accept that some might doubt my experience, I believe God opens our eyes for His purpose. The mere fact of Jesus standing before me was incredible and unexpected, but there He stood and all I could focus on were His eyes. They held me mesmerized and I was filled with warmth and calm. I do not remember the color or shape of those eyes, but I will never forget the incredible, all-encompassing kindness. It was the only word that came to mind as I sat enfolded in a depth of love I had never before experienced. Jesus spoke softly and clearly with heartfelt compassion. He had only one question and I could see He felt the weight of my answer before I gave it.

"What do you want, Brenda, my will or yours?"

The words I knew I must say fought their way up my throat and stuck like a wad of cotton. I could feel myself choking on the surrender I must give. I wanted my will, in the worst way, in the biggest way, more than anything in the world, I wanted my son back. I wanted him to walk through my door. I mentally bargained that if God would bring back my son, I would praise Him, I would make sure everyone knew it was God, I would glorify His name.

"Oh, God. You brought back your Son; can't you bring back mine?" I pleaded.

I knew in that moment I would accept God's will, but I had to ask. I am human, after all.

After my final plea, with tears subsiding as I sat staring at those incredibly kind eyes, a quiet but confident voice from inside me answered, "Yours."

It was not the first time I had surrendered my will to His for this child, but this time the surrender was understood and acknowledged for exactly what I had just done. I was giving up all control, giving up my own will and asking God to carry out His will for my son's life. I knew without one doubt, if God wanted to raised Nick from his place on that gurney and probably cause a heart attack for that medical examiner, He could do it. I also knew that if it was God's will that Nick go home to Heaven that very day, I would not barter for more time. For the first time in those three days of pure emotional brokenness, I managed a weak but genuine smile. His will was my will and I knew it was the only right answer. My son was His first.

Chris, many weeks later would ask me, "Mom, why haven't you ever been mad at God?"

My reply was simple and sincere, "Chris, you and your brothers and sisters were given to me as gifts. I can't look at God and tell Him his gift or the time I was allowed to enjoy that gift is not perfect."

Chris, in all humanness, as a brother missing his brother so much, leaned down and whispered in my ear, "Want me to tell Him?"

Laughing, I assured Chris God and I had certainly had our fair share of "conversations" on the subject. Losing a child is devastating, it defies what we expect, it leaves an indelible imprint for the rest of life. Losing a child was what I once believed to be my greatest fear; however, after losing my precious, precious Nick, I realized, in fact, that was not my greatest fear. My greatest fear would be losing a child and not knowing with certainty that child had accepted salvation and now sat with Jesus.

Later that same third day after my encounter with Jesus I received a text message from a trusted friend and prayer partner.

"I just had to let you know. I saw Nick today in my prayer time. He is sitting with Jesus." Through the tears, I smiled. God was showing up once again, assuring my tattered heart. It was not goodbye.

7

Celebrating Nick

"But those who hope in the Lord will renew their strength. They will soar on wings like eagles; they will run and not grow weary; they will walk and not be faint."
Isaiah 40:31

This is My Song

The week passed with family and friends driving from distances to be with us and the first unexplainable signs of Nick reminders began to show up. As people came and went, our immediate family was at the house most of the time.

The morning after the accident, Chris, Mitch, Jeremy and Travis went to clean out Nick's pickup that had been hauled to town. They brought a few things they would keep and gave me his cell phone, his glasses and his last can of chewing tobacco (chew). I did tell you, Nick was an ordinary guy, right, with his own share of vices? I laid the glasses and phone on my dresser along with the can of chew, right side up.

Throughout that week, the glasses began to take on a life of their own. Every time I or someone would come into my room, the glasses would be in a different position.

Given the many people floating through the house during that time, it could easily have been someone inadvertently moving them. However, one afternoon I had just come from my bedroom and had made sure the glasses were placed upright on the dresser. Niccole was outside waiting to use the bathroom off my bedroom. When she came out, she commented that she had to turn the glasses upright.

I turned and stared at her, "I just made sure they were upright before you went in there!"

Again, I make no profession of knowledge of exactly how the afterlife works. I do however, firmly believe God can do anything, including moving glasses on a dresser. And again, I smiled.

On Friday, January 15, 2016, we honored Nick at a celebration of his life. It is funny the words that became unspeakable to me when speaking of Nick's passing. I could not say the words *die, dead* or *death, funeral* or *obituary* when it was in reference to Nick. I struggle to even write them.

All of those words carried a negative, hopeless darkness to me, and I was desperate to seek purpose, life and meaning. I needed to know my son's passing was part of God's great plan, that it was part of a bigger picture that I just could not see. Perhaps it was also my human mind seeking gentler words to soften the jagged edges of loss. I

IT'S NOT GOODBYE

could say *passed, went home, was received, celebration of life, story of his life, his story,* but not those brutal words that spoke finality. Three years later, those words still offend my tongue and I shy from them like a blistering cup of hot coffee.

Regardless of the words I used or didn't use to describe the situation I had been thrust in, I knew that my saving Grace and my hope would rest in holding on tightly to my faith as thin as that tether might be. That being said, I would also learn, that road of steadfast faith would be far from easy.

At Nick's visitation we greeted hundreds of people, all there to show their respect and offer their condolences. At his service, our large church sanctuary was full to the brim, with some people standing in hallways and any extra rooms available.

I spoke at that service, words that were given to me only hours before it began.

Some people couldn't believe I could speak at my own son's celebration of life. Standing before those who had taken time out of their day to be there for Nick and our family, I couldn't imagine not taking that last time to honor him. While I spoke about my little boy, my grown son and shared precious family memories and things Nick loved; I knew the most important thing I could do to honor Nick was to share what Nick had found in those final months of his life.

These were the words I spoke at the celebration of Nick's life:

"I prayed for God to give me just the right words today. In His perfect timing, He woke me at 3:48

a.m. (coincidence or God? – refer to page 41) and it all came to me. I begin with the book, 'Love You Forever.' It is a book I read often to my five children."

As the story reads, it follows the life of a baby son growing into a man. It is a story of life with babies, toddlers, teenagers and the circle of love between a parent and a child. I may have been reading that book to a packed church, but in my heart, I was simply reading it one last time to my five children, my most precious blessings, together.

As I continued, I looked at faces in the crowd – family, close friends, neighbors, friends of my sons I didn't know and people who came from all distances. How could a thirty-year-old man have touched so many lives that they would take time out of their day to celebrate his life? I was humbled and honored as the words flowed easily.

"Nearly 31 years ago, God gave us a marvelous, marvelous gift, a little boy much like the one in this book. We named him Nicholas Daniel. As an infant he was sweet and cuddly, as a toddler he certainly made his share of messes, in his teenage years, a zoo would have correctly described our household of five children, a mom a dad and an occasional dog, and as Nick grew and he grew, he became a man. And no matter what, I would most definitely still take that grown man and hold him in my arms and I will forever hear that sweet lullaby playing in my mind.

"That, my precious family and friends, is a big love. With big love there is a price, because loving big also hurts big. I remember Nick, who loved big, saying to me only a couple of months before his accident, "I wish I didn't have your heart, mom, then it wouldn't hurt so bad."

I smiled because I understood, but replied, "Never wish away God's gift of big love, Nick. I promise the love is worth the hurt."

(As with so much that happened after losing Nick, I've never stopped believing those words. Even if I had known that I would lose Nick after only 30 years, I still wouldn't have traded the love.)

I continued to speak, "As Nick grew in his relationship with God, as he traveled through his valley and searched for his mountaintop, Nick's heart for Jesus grew as well. He was becoming that warrior for God he had longed to be. In his own perfectly imperfect, ordinary human way, he was becoming that warrior. And in His perfect, extraordinary way, God was leading Nick home."

My concluding sentence was this, "If Nick could tell you anything today, it would be this: Get to know my God."

I kissed my son for the last time, tucked the book beneath his folded arms and whispered, "See ya later."

The house became empty, leftover food was thrown out, the many flowers began to wilt and the thank you cards were almost all sent out. While Grace still covered my ragged heart and reality remained blurred, the fog was beginning to clear and I realized…this is my life. And I began to grieve…

8

Grief

But He said to me, 'My Grace is made sufficient for you, for my power is made perfect in weakness..."
2 Corinthians 12:9

Grief has been perceived as a finite period of time, a journey to a destination. However, destination implies an end, and grief truly has no decisive end.

Grief has also been described as a "natural emotional response to the loss of someone or something that is loved." I would agree. It is emotions on steroids, emotions run amok, emotions overflowing.

The first twelve months after losing Nick was the year we came to call our "year of firsts." The first overwhelming, aftermath wave of grief to hit me, occurred late one night as I sat on my bed, alone for the first time. I was surrounded by boxes of pictures that just weeks before my girls and our go-to video creator had so carefully woven into a video remembrance of Nick for his funeral services.

IT'S NOT GOODBYE

That night the grief came gently, a simple melancholy that swept over me as I sifted through the years. With each tender memory, the ache began to swell. The tears rushed faster, and the sobs became screams that lasted until I was fully spent. Thankfully it was winter and the windows were closed.

Sitting motionless in my cross-legged position, I glimpsed headlights pull into my driveway. Looking at the clock, I saw it was 11:00 p.m. Who would be coming here at this hour? I could tell it was a pickup but didn't recognize the shape of the person in the dark shadows as they got out and headed for my front door. I wiped away the tears, knowing I must look like a ragged mess and tentatively rounded the corner to see Nick's best friend, Shaun, standing at the doorway. My heart jumped with relief as he opened the door and I gave him a big hug.

"What are you doing here?" I asked, not surprised that it was Shaun. He and Nick were the best of friends and through the years, the two of them had often dropped by unexpectedly just to visit.

Shaun looked at me and answered, "It was the weirdest thing. I was working in the field [Shaun is a farmer] and I was trying to get done, but I kept hearing a voice telling me I needed to come see you."

I stood there grinning and shaking my head in wonder.

"Nick sent you," I said.

Shaun smiled back and shook his own head.

"I knew it was late," he said, "but I couldn't get that nagging feeling to go away. I finally just stopped and drove over here."

I invited Shaun in, and we sat and talked…about Nick. I wanted to hear all the stories I had never heard. Some stories I was thankful I had not known before (I did mention Nick was every bit a fun lover?) and some I was so thankful to hear for the first time. This was a trusted friend of Nick's and he could share parts of Nick I hadn't known. With Nick gone, I was desperate to know everything, to amass all the memories I could and store them for the dark and lonely moments I somehow knew would come. Talking to Shaun was a connection to Nick and a comfort, but more importantly, it was the beginning of my quest to understand.

I had hoped we would receive messages from God. I wanted to believe that God would send signs, like a cardinal, pennies, butterflies, feathers, friends at just the right time. I wanted to know everything about the afterlife, because heaven was now personal and more real than it had ever been to me. I needed the assurance of God's promises. I needed the scripture that clarified what I had been taught.

"I desire to depart and be with Christ, which is better by far."
Philippians 1:23

As a believer, according to this word, Nick now sat with Jesus just as my friend had revealed. Believing that Nick sits with God, in whatever form our spirit/soul/essence takes on, I leave open the endless possibilities to hear from God and in some way know that they are reminders of Nick and his eternity.

While the grief was still new and tender, I needed a purpose to get up, to get dressed and to "get on," as much as I didn't want to, "with life." I began to dig deeper into the Bible and scripture.

I found comfort in finding out everything about where Nick was now, but I can't pretend the grief just went away or that it was easier. Oddly enough as time passed, grief did become not only a familiar but a strangely welcome visitor. To grieve was to feel and to feel was to live.

One thing I recognized early on was that Satan loves what hurts humans most. He relishes the opportunity to turn us from God and will use anything to his advantage. His purpose is to ***"steal, kill and destroy…"* John 10:10** and he made no exception for me.

After my first encounter with grief that came gently and comforted, the *what ifs?*— "What if I had been there? What if I had convinced Nick not to go that night? What if I hadn't almost insisted he come home? What if it had not been January and bitter cold? What if someone had found him sooner?" and the *Whys?*— "Why when Nick had just been growing so strong in faith? Why at thirty when he had so much life left to live? Why when life was just getting good again?"— began to attack randomly and viciously. The *"If onlys"* chimed in as well with the same assaulting words.

Those words were accusing, and guilt ridden. I recognized the source, I knew in my head where the fear and doubt were coming from, but it didn't stop my heart from asking the agonizing questions or beating myself up emotionally. I was supposed to fix things, take care of things, take care of my kids, and I felt like a failure as a parent. My biggest job, the one I strove to do the very best, I had failed at it. And how Satan must have loved those thoughts.

Satan is a wily opponent and loves to attack when we are most vulnerable, but over the course of a few weeks I did one day stand my ground. On that day, I raised my hand in the air, all alone in my living room and boldly banished Satan from my house, from my family and the defeating thoughts from my head. I might also have scared anyone coming to my door!

"You have no place here, Satan. You will not win, we will not turn away," I cried at the top of my voice, "I call on the name of Jesus!"

I can't say that was the last time Satan tried to attack my fragile emotions or that I was always so good at remembering where the negative thoughts and feelings came from. It was a constant battle and some days I was strong and some days I wasn't. It was my new life, I was surviving, but the ache didn't go away and the missing Nick did not get less. What got me through it? Friends, family, prayer and most of all—God. He was simply always there.

9

A Year of Firsts

"My flesh and my heart may fail, but God is the strength of my heart and my portion forever."
Psalms 73:26

And so began our first year after Nick's passing. The first big "first" was Nick's birthday. I wrote him a letter and sealed it in an envelope. It might sound strange to hear I wrote my customary birthday letter now that Nick was gone, but as you see, I don't rule out anything God can do, including reading a letter written on earth to my son in Heaven. Friends and family gathered at my house to remember him. We shared food and drinks (doesn't every Midwest gathering include these two things?) and "Nick" stories. It was healing and comforting to be with friends and family as we navigated this new normal.

This first birthday where we celebrated Nick's birthday without Nick was also one of the first times in several years that we hadn't celebrated our two March birthdays, Nick and his nephew, Trenton together. Before those two birthdays that year, I worried how we would still make it a good birthday for Trenton. That was the year that we celebrated Nick on the 3rd (his actual birthdate) and Trenton had his own birthday gathering. It became important to not only recognize the grief my own kids were experiencing, but to also be aware that Nick had six young nephews who were missing him, too and trying to cope with the loss, as kids. I would learn to balance the focus on Nick with equal and eventually more focus on Niccole, Chris, Mitch, Jordyn and their families. I couldn't lose myself so deep in grief that I sacrificed or wasted the time I had with these four left here on earth and their families.

Between the "firsts" of that year, I struggled through grieving the loss of Nick and aching equally, if not more, as I watched the sorrow of my sons and daughters. Close families have strong and lasting bonds not only as family but as friends.

Chris and Nick had worked side by side since Nick turned 18. Mitch had worked alongside them for only a short time but had always looked up to and spent a lot of time with his brothers as he got older. They were not only brothers but friends, the "Grose brothers" as they were called. The hole left by Nick's passing was agonizing for his two best friend/brothers.

Nick's sisters Niccole and Jordyn each shared their own special connection. Niccole found friendship, a listening ear and a counselor in her younger brother and Jordyn was quite simply the female version of Nick! She and Nick were compadres, confidantes and friends.

Each of my children grieved differently. With the support of their spouses, each found different avenues to navigate their own new normal as they all grieved together.

As a mom, I tried to keep my own feelings contained and offer support when we were together. I believed I needed to be strong for them knowing and understanding I couldn't lean on them, just yet; they were hurting themselves. Besides, caring for them was what I had always done, it was familiar and much easier than focusing on my own grief. I was also committed to not only being strong for my children, but to show them God's Grace, His love and to use Nick's passing as an opportunity to point them toward understanding their own gift of salvation.

As for my own stronghold here on earth, I had the outlet of wonderful friends who were always there for me—to listen, to give a hug, a tissue or a girl's day out. My heavenly stronghold also never failed me. The comfort I found from knowing with certainty that Nick sat with Jesus was indescribable. On my worst days and my best days, I held tight to God's promises about His constant love, our eternal salvation and Heaven.

In my early searches of the Bible, I found sixteen scriptures about the promise of Heaven that I clung to. As I continued to seek knowledge, assurance and comfort, I found even more and each one lifted me up from the darkness into a state of what I might call, "joy in the mourning." It was unexplainable and sometimes I almost felt guilty for the joy that came with the same unexpected arrival as the waves of grief.

If you are like me and are searching for answers, for assurance and reassurance in the loss of a loved one, I have shared several scriptures throughout this book, but there are so many more! Find them and cling to them!

These scriptures became my strength and a fortress for my mind, ready to call on at a moment's notice. I had to be equipped and on alert. Satan was always lurking to catch me in a weak or doubting moment and there were plenty of those days. I knew my best armor was the word of God.

Slowly, as the weeks passed, although I didn't want to believe time would "soften" the grief, it did. There were still the times spent crying stuffed deep in the darkness of my closet, the times when I would sit holding "Nick" (the smoothly polished walnut box that served as his urn) for comfort, times when I would spend hours looking through pictures, times when the family would get together and share stories and tears and the ache would feel just as fresh. There were still days when I sat in numbed silence and the pain screamed loudly in my head and there were times when I couldn't stay busy enough…as though I could outrun the feelings or push them deep beneath the methodical swoosh of the vacuum cleaner. And there were the days I wrote incessantly. Journaling was cathartic to me. Just putting the words on paper would sometimes smooth the roughness of the reality that life here would no longer include Nick.

Mitch and Erica's wedding came (our second "first") on April 9 of that year. Mitch had chosen Chris and Nick as his two groomsmen and was not replacing Nick, so the order of the wedding procession was ad-libbed. Chris walked in two beautiful bridesmaids, one on each arm and a plaque for Nick sat discreetly in the pew nearby.

Nick's presence was missed, every second of that day, but this day was not a celebration of Nick - this was a celebration of Mitch and Erica's marriage. And so, we danced, we laughed, we celebrated and of course, we told Nick stories. At the end of the night, our family gathered in a circle for the playing of the last song, "You Should Be Here" by Cole Swindell.

I think we will always think of Nick at those moments, and I don't believe the tears will ever end, but they became mixed with joy that day and as each new "first" arrived we would grieve, and we would remember. Eventually the remembering began to bring smiles and a few less tears. Grief doesn't follow a timetable and the stages of grief are not experienced in order, but grief is a process of time and time was passing as much as we had once thought it should stand still.

While I mentioned my desire to share the messages of salvation with my children, that passion at times became almost an obsession. I felt driven to not fail with such an important mission. My sometimes-overzealous approach could easily be analyzed by a psychologist or even by someone with a psychology degree, like me. I still fought the feelings of failing Nick, as incorrect as they were, and I needed to not fail these four I still had here on earth.

God used this newfound zest to share the amazing gift Nick had received with others, by giving me a fresh boldness in faith. I was no longer afraid of offending man but became very concerned about offending God. My passion extended beyond my immediate family and later, that first year after Nick's passing, to my non-believing (at the time) brother, Dan.

Around May of that year, Dan lay on an emergency examination table, waiting for a critical surgery that he might or might not survive.

I had promised if God allowed me to get to my brother's bedside before he went into surgery, I would witness to him. It was a tall order and a big promise. Dan was scientific thinking and professed he lacked belief in God. Life hadn't always been kind to Dan, Dan hadn't always been kind to life, and I suspect my brother with the great big heart had maybe felt let down too many times and perhaps given up on God.

I made it in time, opportunity (or God?) presented itself, and as I stood at my brother's bedside, I began by posing this question, "What if a store was offering an amazing gift for free? What if all you had to do to get the gift was ask for it? What if I knew about that gift, and went and received it for myself, but didn't let you know anything about it? What kind of sister would I be?"

He smiled at me, as I went on and simply replied, "Oh, sis, I'll be okay," but seeing the tears in my eyes, he continued, "but if it means that much to you, okay."

I wasn't sure at the time he completely believed me, but it got him thinking and that was enough. I knew I wasn't just speaking my opinion about salvation, **Romans 6:23** says it in nearly those same words. *"For the wages of sin is death, but the free gift of God is eternal life in Christ Jesus our Lord."*

God's word is straightforward. We are sinners, but Jesus paid our bill. It is free! I had shared the message; God would do the "heart work".

And just like He did! Only a few months later as Dan faced his fading health battling stage 4 cancer and the end of his days here on earth (save a miracle) I knew he had heard my words.

He looked at me on one of my visits and with an accepting grin he said, "You know, Sis, I bet there aren't many non-believers in a foxhole."

I bet there aren't, Dan. My brother passed away in December of that year, having accepted Jesus as His Savior. I kept my promise to God and God opened my brother's eyes in his last days.

You've probably figured it out by now…God was there and we were beginning to recognize His presence more quickly. God was determined we would understand, this life is not all there is and He showed us at every turn, it's not goodbye.

Our third "first" was connected to Nick's love of competition. In 2015, JNC Construction -- Chris, Jared, Nick, and Mitch -- had spent donated time and equipment restoring a small little league field in the tiny town of Clearfield, IA, twenty miles west of Mt. Ayr. When the job was complete, the boys started hitting balls. Always one up for competition, Nick swung for the fence and, of course, the ball sailed over.

In Summer 2016 we held the first annual "Nick Grose Memorial Homerun Derby." It was a brainchild of Chris Leonard, Jared Mains, and my sons Mitch and Chris. It seemed fitting that Nick be remembered by a sport he loved at a field he had helped restore in a town he loved.

The first year attracted a small gathering of people. It rained and only the true-blue friends and family stuck around to the conclusion. We raised a good amount of money, and we began planning what project we would fund each year in our community. The tears fell that night, "Nick stories" were told (there are far more than I knew) and another first had passed. We were remembering Nick in all the best ways and we were still surviving (is there any other word for it?) our first year.

I mentioned earlier in the book that Nick's desire was to lead his brothers to a deeper understanding and faith in God. God began that work in Chris on a warm summer day in June of that first year when Chris crawled into the "dozer" that had been "Nick's."

The first time he had to run that piece of equipment was hard for Chris, memories flooded and I'm sure the "you should be heres." He missed his brother most on those days that were days they had shared so often in the past.

IT'S NOT GOODBYE

That day as Chris shifted the gears and began his day's work, he turned on the radio for company. It was Sunday and the only radio station that came in as he worked in that isolated farm field was a church service broadcast from an area church. Chris listened (he had no other choice- a sermon or the steady hum of the machine) and as he listened, he became attentive. This guy was talking about stuff that just couldn't be wrong. His case for God was clear and there could be no other answer. It was scientific and beyond error. God had to exist! I don't know the exact message, but a few weeks later, the impact on Chris was clear as he and I were visiting.

Chris recalled that day in the dozer, listening to the pastor and how it all made sense to him.

"Remember when I always agreed with you when you talked about God?" he began.

"Yes?" I replied unsure where the conversation was going.

"I just told you what you wanted to hear," he admitted, "but I want you to know now, I do believe." My son of few words gave me a quiet grin and ended the conversation.

I looked at him and smiled. As Nick's heart had aligned with God's, God now would do the work Nick had so longed for. I whispered a breath prayer of thankfulness.

God's work in Mitch came in a much different way. He had been my two-year-old who sat rapt at the feet of our pastor every Sunday morning and then would later go home to deliver sermons to the family (and we all had to sit down and listen). I had never wondered about where Mitch stood on the subject of God.

Mitch however, like everyone had his share of mixed emotions after losing Nick. At one moment he was standing strong in faith and in another, the ache of losing Nick would take over and he would be angry. I don't know that he was or was not mad at God, but he didn't understand why he had to lose his brother and he catapulted 0-10 through his feelings and his beliefs.

One night our family had all gathered for a barbecue and hanging in Mitch's garage. Everyone was gone but me. Often those "just Mitch and I" moments were times when we talked a lot about

Nick and missing him. That night Mitch was looking for a song to play on his phone.

"Remember that song about blessings and raindrops that we had played at Nick's service?" He asked.

"'Blessings' by Laura Story?" I asked.

"Yeah, that one," Mitch replied as he Googled it and then instructed "Alexa" to play it.

As it played, Mitch sang along, knowing all the words. He knew every word. The song talked about blessings and how they might sometimes be disguised as raindrops and about healing disguised as tears. It was obvious he had listened to it before and he understood the significance of the words. Our raindrops were being revealed as blessings and our healing was coming through many tears. Mitch had not completely worked through his confusion and his doubts, but it was obvious this song had reached out to him. As with each time I saw God's hand at work, I smiled and I was humbled. I could not completely fathom the *whys* for the love God was showing, my very ordinary family, my very perfectly imperfect, ordinary family, but I was so very thankful.

Although we would travel through the rollercoaster of emotions and the healing had only begun, I continually marveled at that handprint of God's work.

I was learning that Nick would touch lives, in our small community and states away, through conversation, or the retelling of his story, because of the love and Grace of God. By Nick's example of growing love for God, by the certain saving of that ordinary, perfectly human, vices and all, son—Nick would indeed lead his brothers and sisters into a greater understanding of faith and God.

That, however, did not stop the ache of missing Nick, the sadness for the *"should have beens"* and the brokenness from our forever-missing piece. Our grief continued, but we were still surviving…as always by the Grace of God.

As the six-month mark approached, I began to feel like I should be in a "progressed" state of grief. I felt the expectation for "moving on" and that I should be "healing." When waves of huge grief swept over me…whether for days or weeks or a moment, I felt weak, as though I wasn't being "good" enough or strong enough for God and all those who watched my journey.

I began to limit the times I would honestly share my feelings or thoughts with friends. I thought I was beyond the time of active grieving and they would surely be tired of me, as though it was time to "get over it", as though it was nothing more than a bad cold.

I didn't want to worry my friends or family if I shared those intense dark moments that still came out of nowhere and I didn't want to make them feel bad. I put timetables on myself based on what I thought were societal expectations even though I knew, grief has no rules.

I also feared people would see me as broken in need of fixing. I didn't think I needed fixing, in fact, I didn't want to be fixed. I needed to feel and I needed to be heard and be validated. I needed to know my feelings were mine and it was okay to feel them. I felt alone a lot, even in a group and pretending was so exhausting. Sometimes isolation beckoned like a warm cocoon. I began to seek it more often than I should have and continued to wear my brave face.

In truth, my brave face was not fooling my closest friends or family. They did not put expectations on me and fully supported my need to grieve in whatever way and for as much time as I needed, including forever. They didn't believe me for a minute when I said, "I'm fine" and they didn't miss the sudden glisten of tears that came often and at times even surprised me. Those friends and family supported me through loss before Nick's passing and never would they have judged or rejected my needs. Did I mention, I am blessed by the most amazing family and friends?

I was also not ever really alone. God was there, even when I did not cry out or acknowledge Him, and those friends and family were always only a phone call or a short drive away. The fear, I recognized, was my own and Satan was feeding that fire. God's word reminded me, ***"Put on the full armor of God, so that you may fight against the devil's schemes."*** **Ephesians 6:11**

Loss of a loved one is a vulnerable time for anyone and Satan is good at knowing just when to whisper his words of doubt and fear. God, however, knows our hearts even more intimately, and He rose up bigger and stronger every time Satan tried to attack my wounded heart.

"So do not fear, for I am with you, do not be dismayed, for I am your God. I will strengthen you and help you. I will uphold you with my righteous right hand." Isaiah 41:10

And just as His word says, God WAS there.

One morning it was one of those "grief wave" days, the ones that hit you in the face out of nowhere and you are a mess. I had been cleaning my room and had cleaned off a dresser I was taking to the garage. After finishing cleaning and vacuuming my room I jumped in the shower. The tears began to flow, and I was praying and crying and showering. I was grieving so big and so hard.

I missed Nick, I believed and trusted with absolute certainty that Nick was in Heaven, but it just wasn't soothing my heart that day. I needed reassurance, I needed God to hear me and answer me as I pled my heart out to Him.

As I stepped from the shower, I looked over at the dresser in my bathroom I had just dusted. Laying on top of that just cleaned surface was a bright shiny penny. Right in the middle of that dresser I had cleaned and dusted only minutes before jumping in the shower lay that penny, shining bright. I stood there staring at it before picking it up and closing it gently in my hand.

No one was at home but me, there could be no other explanation. God had heard my pleas and

He had answered. It was a first, but it would not be the last.

We have come to call them Nick pennies, and they show up on garage floors, freshly washed counters, just vacuumed rugs, on a sidewalk you have just walked down and always they come with no other possible, logical explanation for their appearance but God.

We have come to understand and accept when we need to hear from Nick, however it works between Heaven and earth, God answers that call. I don't know why or how, but I do know He always answers.

Time continued to pass in that first year and it was soon December and it was our first Christmas without Nick. The first thing to clutch my heart was the stockings as I unpacked them from one of my green and red totes. There was Nick's stocking. The tears gushed. I couldn't put it back in the tote, but I couldn't hang it as I always had with all the family stockings. I held that stocking and sobbed for quite some time, alone with my tender memories. I hung the others and laid the single stocking that read, Nick, at the end of the stair banister. I needed to hang it up, but how and where?

I decided to create Nick's own Christmas corner, not front and center, but with three small trees I decorated with all of his childhood ornaments and his stocking. It was perfect. The tears dried and again I found a smile.

On Christmas Eve as I filled the other thirteen stockings with the expected array of socks, colognes, small games and candy, I knew Nick's stocking should hold something just for him. Going to my room, I went to my miniature keepsake chest and pulled out the folded letters I had written to Nick through the years. I stuck them clear to the bottom of the stocking (this was just between us) but I wanted to somehow believe he would read them and know how much I loved him and how very much I missed him.

We chose "Christmas Vacation," a Grose classic favorite, as our theme for Pajama Night. Mitch showed up winning the best costume for his "Cousin Eddy" impersonation, friends thought of us and stopped by and brought special keepsake ornaments, and we did take that annual family picture although I think we all knew our hearts weren't quite in it that year.

IT'S NOT GOODBYE

It wasn't the same, we were beginning to realize it would never be the same, but our year of firsts was nearly over, and we had survived, as a family. But more than survival, we had cried out in desperate need and aching heartbreak and God was there, bigger, bolder and more merciful than we had ever imagined. Every single time, He was there.

10

Hello, Last First

"But those who hope in the Lord will renew their strength. They will soar on wings like eagles; they will run and not grow weary; they will walk and not be faint."
Isaiah 40:31

Praising my Savior, all the Day Long.

On January 10, 2017, I wrote:

"Hello, last first,

We meet at last. I knew this day would come, but I didn't know how I would feel, what I would do or how I would react when you finally arrived.

I gave myself permission to give this day to Nick. I stayed in bed, huddled in my fleece pjs and an old blanket and I remembered. I finally watched the video that had stayed untouched in its jacket since the funeral and I laughed at Nick wearing a pair of underwear on his head, Nick cutting up, Nick with his arm slung confidently around a shoulder, Nick and his buddies, Nick and his family, Nick living life.

IT'S NOT GOODBYE

I meandered down the road of memories and realized the smiles now come more often than the tears. The ache of loss is still vivid, the number of times I think of Nick are not fewer, but my heart has begun to heal.

There will always be a hole in that heart, but someone once told me, instead of thinking of it as empty with loss, look at the hole as filled with the thirty years of Nick.

In a year, I have been blessed to see the purpose in God's timing. I have witnessed the Grace of God and have received the signs I longed for that remind me, he is not gone, but simply waiting beyond that which separates Heaven and Earth.

Along the way, I have also learned humility, faithfulness, obedience and submission to God's will and a few things about life:

- We are here for God's purpose, not our own. Seek His Will
- Eliminate the stuff that clutters life
- Prioritize that which is most important and give it your best attention
- Laugh a lot….and often….
- Watch a sun set, really watch it as it slides into the horizon and tell me….is that not God?
- Yes, take that trip, eat that cake, and buy those shoes, in other words…don't wait for tomorrow to live your best life.
- Sit out at that baseball/softball game or football game in the rain and smile knowing

that son or daughter, that grandson or granddaughter looks into the stands and knows you are there

- ❖ Climb mountains if you will, go white water rafting, parasailing or zip lining…have an adventure
- ❖ Play 100 games of Go Fish with a 7-year-old and keep smiling
- ❖ Sweep the dirt and fold the laundry and be thankful for life in the house
- ❖ Eat chocolate
- ❖ Watch endless episodes of ABC kids until you know all the words and be thankful for the little one who introduced you again to the simplicity of toddler life
- ❖ Embrace your valleys, it is there you truly see the face of God.

- ❖ Choose a small and trusted circle and spend your time wisely with those you love, who love you right back
- ❖ Never apologize for your heart or your feelings
- ❖ Love wholly, love unconditionally, love intentionally
- ❖ Life is temporary, Heaven is eternal…choose wisely your destination.
- ❖ And foremost, never forget…It's not goodbye.

As I wept long into the night, God was there. As I longed for just one more day or one more hour, God understood. As I searched for answers, God provided them. When I was weak, God was my strength. When I wanted to give up, God told me to hang on. When I thought I couldn't take another step, God picked me up. When I found my passion to share God's amazing Grace, He gave me the words.

As Nick's story unfolded, God's presence was revealed, from the very first minute he took his first breath until the moment he breathed his last. In every step along the way of Nick's life we saw God revealed, sometimes as it happened and sometimes as we look back.

What we learned as a family after Nick's passing was that God never leaves, he waits to welcome us home. Death is not a tragedy for God but a homecoming for his children. We learned to cling to God's many promises throughout that first incredibly tough, aching, raw, sensitive rollercoaster of a ride through loss. And the promise that kept us going? the promise that renewed our spirits and lightened our hearts? was the promise that truly, "It's Not Goodbye". To that I can only offer a humble thank you, Jesus for your work on the cross and to Nick, "we'll see ya later."

"May the words of my mouth and the meditations of my heart, be pleasing in your sight, Oh Lord, my Rock and my Redeemer."
Psalms 19:14

About the Author

Brenda Grose is an "always work in progress" Christian, a mom to three sons and two daughters and Gram to seven amazing grandsons. She is a life-long writer and after the loss of her son in 2016, found a passion to share the message of God's Grace experienced first-hand on her journey through grief. Brenda is a public speaker and beginning blogger with a website devoted to reaching out to others experiencing loss. She lives in Mount Ayr, Iowa and welcomes the opportunity to travel to share her story.

Website: www.hearttoheartamothersjourney.com
Email: hearttoheartamothersjourney@gmail.com
Twitter: @BrendaKGrose

Made in the USA
Columbia, SC
23 June 2019